AF575376

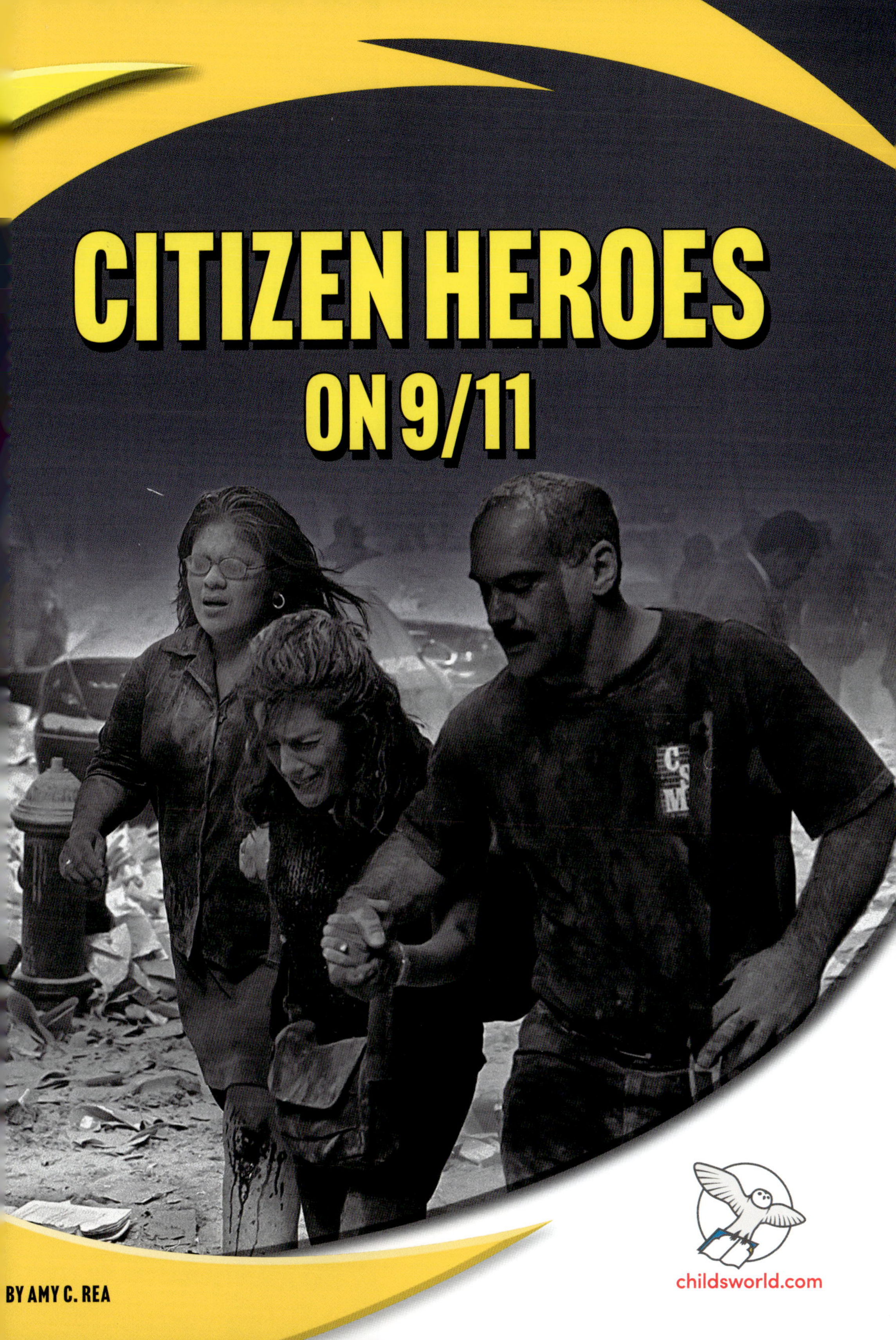

CITIZEN HEROES
ON 9/11
BY AMY C. REA
childsworld.com

Published by The Child's World®
800-599-READ • www.childsworld.com

Photography Credits
Photographs ©: Gulnara Samoilova/AP Images, cover, 1; James Radja/Shutterstock Images, 5; Chang W. Lee/Getty Images News/Getty Images, 6; Richard Drew/Getty Images News/Getty Images, 9; Maddie Meyer/Getty Images Sport/Getty Images, 10; Anna Moneymaker/Getty Images News/Getty Images, 12; US Air Force, 14; Spc. April York/DVIDS, 15; Petty Officer 1st Class Molly Burgess/US Navy/DVIDS, 17; Danny Johnston/AP Images, 18; iStockphoto, 20; Shutterstock Images, 22 (planes); Red Line Editorial, 22 (buildings); Gene J. Puskar/AP Images, 23; Petty Officer 1st Class Brien Aho/US Navy/DVIDS, 24; Senior Master Sgt. Kevin J. Gruenwald/US Air Force/DVIDS, 26; Stephen Hassay/US Navy/DVIDS, 27; Grant Greenwalt/US Department of Defense, 28

ISBN Information
9781503889101 (Reinforced Library Binding)
9781503890848 (Portable Document Format)
9781503892088 (Online Multi-user eBook)
9781503893320 (Electronic Publication)

LCCN 2023950401

Printed in the United States of America

ABOUT THE AUTHOR

Amy C. Rea grew up in northern Minnesota and now lives in a Minneapolis suburb with her family. She writes frequently about traveling around Minnesota and loves spending time with her family and her silly dog.

CONTENTS

FAST FACTS

- On September 11, 2001, **terrorists** took over four airplanes. They crashed two **hijacked** planes into the World Trade Center in New York City. They crashed another into the Pentagon near Washington, DC. Passengers on the fourth plane fought back. That plane crashed into a field in Pennsylvania.
- Welles Crowther worked on the 104th floor of the World Trade Center's South Tower. He helped people escape before the tower collapsed.
- Marilyn Wills was at the Pentagon when the plane hit. She carried another woman on her back to safety.
- Tom Burnett was on United Airlines Flight 93 flying from New Jersey to California when it was hijacked. He and the other passengers learned about the other terrorist attacks. They worked together to stop the hijackers of their plane.
- Merwynn Pagdanganan worked in information technology (IT) at the Pentagon. When a plane crashed into the Pentagon, he helped many people escape.

A national memorial honoring Flight 93 was built in the Shanksville, Pennsylvania, field where the plane crashed. The Tower of Voices at the memorial is 93 feet (28.3 m) tall. It contains 40 wind chimes to honor the 40 victims.

CHAPTER ONE

WELLES CROWTHER

Welles Crowther was at work on September 11, 2001. He worked in the World Trade Center's South Tower in New York City. A plane had hit the North Tower several minutes earlier. Crowther had felt and heard it. His friend John Howells called him to ask if he was OK. Crowther said he was, but he needed to go. People in the building were telling everyone to leave.

But just after 9 a.m., he heard an enormous bang. It sounded like an explosion. The building began to sway. United Airlines Flight 175 had crashed into the South Tower. The plane hit between the 77th and 85th floors. Crowther worked on the 104th floor.

The building began to fill with smoke. When Crowther was a child, his father gave him a red bandanna to keep in his back pocket. From then on, he always carried a red bandanna with him.

A photo of Welles Crowther and his mother, Alison, is shown at the 2014 dedication of the National September 11 Memorial Museum.

It helped him feel closer to his father. A coworker had asked him about the bandanna once. He told her it would change the world someday. Crowther wrapped it around his nose and mouth to avoid inhaling too much smoke. Then he went down to the lobby of the 78th floor.

There were many people in the lobby. Some were crying. Others were shouting. Many were injured, and some were dead. The elevators did not work. Crowther could tell that people were panicking. Crowther had been a **volunteer** firefighter as a teenager. He had been thinking about quitting his job to become a full-time firefighter. He knew from his training that it was important to stay calm. They all needed to find a way out.

Crowther started looking for a fire extinguisher. He told people about a nearby staircase. He said that anyone who could walk should go down it now. Anyone who could help others could try to find someone and lead them down, too. Ling Young was one of the people in the 78th floor's lobby. Crowther guided her to the staircase. He followed her down. Young noticed Crowther was carrying a woman on his back. Crowther stopped at the 61st floor to put her down. The air was clearer here. Crowther told them he was going back up to help more people down.

Ling Young (left) and Alison Crowther (center) speak with President Barack Obama before their speech at the dedication of the National September 11 Memorial Museum.

Welles Crowther was a student athlete at Boston College. The school unveiled special uniforms in 2014 and announced an annual Red Bandanna Game to honor Crowther and other graduates who died in the September 11 attacks.

Crowther later joined a group of firefighters. They had a tool to help people who were trapped. But just before 10 a.m., the building began to shudder and creak, making terrible noises. Then it collapsed. Crowther's body was later found in the South Tower's lobby with the firefighters. They were close to the exit. But they had not been able to escape.

The survivors whom Crowther had helped did not know who he was. Months later, the *New York Times* published a story about a man with a red bandanna who had saved people in the South Tower. Crowther's mother saw the story. She knew he always had a red bandanna. She reached out to the survivors from the story and showed them Crowther's photo. He was the hero who had helped save them.

Crowther is an example of a citizen hero. Many police officers, firefighters, and military members are heroes for trying to save and protect others. A citizen hero is someone who tries to save and protect others even though it is not his or her job. Crowther had worked as a volunteer firefighter. He had considered becoming one again. But he was not a firefighter on September 11. He did not have to try to save anyone. He could have escaped the building on his own. Instead, he helped others find a way out. "He was acting as a firefighter at the last hour of his life," Crowther's father said. "He wasn't an **equities trader** anymore. He was a firefighter."

CHAPTER TWO

MARILYN WILLS

Marilyn Wills was at the Pentagon near Washington, DC, on the morning of September 11, 2001. She worked for the US Army. At 9 a.m., she was in a conference room with about a dozen people. They were having a meeting.

In 2021, Marilyn Wills spoke on a panel with other people who were at the Pentagon on September 11, 2001.

Suddenly, there was an intense blast. The lights went out. The force of the blast blew Wills out of her chair and across the table. She was stunned. The building had recently been under construction. She thought the blast may have come from that work. She and her coworkers did not know that American Airlines Flight 77 had just crashed into the Pentagon.

Army employee Philip McNair shouted that everyone needed to leave the room. But the room was dark as night. It was filling with smoke that smelled terrible. No one knew if the building would collapse. Wills crawled to a nearby door. But the door's handle was too hot to touch. She started crawling to the room's other exit. Someone grabbed Wills's leg. It was her coworker, Lois Stevens. Wills told Stevens to hold on. "Where I go, you go," she said. Wills led Stevens out of the room. She realized a group of people were following them.

Wills crawled through smoke and flames. Black smoke was filling everyone's lungs. Stevens stopped crawling. Her pantyhose had melted onto her legs. She said she could not go on. "Oh yes, you can," Wills said. "Just get on my back, I'll carry you." They continued crawling along the floor. The smoke made it very hard to breathe. Then the overhead sprinklers turned on.

Water came down on them as they tried to find a way out. Wills stopped and took off the black wool sweater she wore. Wool absorbs water easily. She took the sweater and soaked it in a puddle on the floor. Then she brought it to her mouth and sucked some of the water from it. It helped her mouth not be as dry from the smoke. Then she passed the wet sweater along to the rest of the group so they could do the same.

THE PENTAGON

Workers began building the Pentagon in 1941. It is made almost completely of reinforced concrete. That means the concrete has steel built into it. The Pentagon was designed to be much stronger than most buildings. Its design kept it from collapsing right away, which allowed more people to escape.

Colonel Marilyn Wills speaks with soldiers in Afghanistan in 2011.

Finally, Wills could see light through a window at the end of the hall. She moved toward it. But the window was built to withstand blasts. It would not break. Another person threw a printer at it. The printer bounced and hit Wills. Wills had brought everyone to the window. Now it wouldn't open. She was afraid they were all going to die. But then someone had an idea.

The group pushed the window out of its frame. They were able to open it enough for people to slide through. They would have to drop 15 feet (4.6 m) to the ground. But Wills felt they had no choice. "Let's get these people out of here," she said.

First responders saw smoke pouring out of the window. They made a human ladder to help everyone down. Each person stood on another person's shoulders until they reached the window. The people in the building were able to climb down. Wills and McNair helped everyone else go through the window. When just the two of them were left, Wills wanted to stay and look for others. But McNair knew it was too dangerous. He ordered Wills to go through the window, too. Once she landed on the ground, she was taken to the hospital to have her burns and smoke **inhalation** treated. She had to stay there nine days. Later, the government awarded Wills a Soldier's Medal for bravery and a Purple Heart for her wounds.

McNair talked about how important Wills's help was. "Some people panic in situations like that," he said. "They scream, lose their cool. Marilyn was calm, collected, thinking quickly. . . . You are in a **foxhole**. It was an honor to be in the foxhole with Marilyn Wills."

At the dedication of the Pentagon Memorial in 2008, 184 service members stood beside the 184 memorial units. These honor the 59 people on American Airlines Flight 77 and 125 people inside the Pentagon who died on September 11, 2001.

CHAPTER THREE

TOM BURNETT

Tom Burnett was in New York City for work. He was flying home to San Francisco, California, on the morning of September 11, 2001. At the airport, he boarded United Airlines Flight 93. The airplane was a Boeing 757. It could hold up to 182 passengers. But that morning's flight had only 33 passengers and seven crew members. It seemed like it would be a quiet flight. But the passengers and crew did not know that there were also four terrorists on board.

Flight 93 departed Newark, New Jersey, for San Francisco. The plane took off at 8:42 a.m., 25 minutes behind schedule. At 8:46 a.m., the first plane crashed into the World Trade Center. But the people on Flight 93 did not know that. At 9:25 a.m., the pilot checked in with an air traffic controller in Cleveland, Ohio. Everything seemed fine.

Deena Burnett and her children hold a photo of Tom Burnett in 2003. Tom died on September 11, 2001.

From the 1980s to the mid-2000s, airplanes often had built-in phones that passengers could use. Passengers on Flight 93 used these phones to contact their loved ones.

But three minutes later, the Cleveland center heard sounds of struggling coming from the cockpit of Flight 93. The plane suddenly dropped almost 700 feet (210 meters). The Cleveland air controller tried to get the pilot to talk to him. No one answered. The hijackers had taken over the plane.

The hijackers forced the passengers and crew to the back of the plane. The crew and passengers began making calls. Burnett called his wife, Deena. He said, "Our airplane has been hijacked. . . . The hijackers have already [stabbed] a guy, . . . they are telling us there is a bomb on board, please call the **authorities**."

Deena called the police right away. Then Burnett called her again. She told him that other planes had been hijacked and crashed into the World Trade Center. Burnett hung up the phone to talk to the other passengers. When he called his wife back again, she told him a plane had crashed into the Pentagon. He told the other passengers. Burnett told his wife he did not think there was really a bomb on board. He thought the hijackers said that to scare the passengers into obeying orders. Burnett said he and other passengers were starting to make a plan.

Other passengers were calling their family members, too. Several of them told their family that the plane had been hijacked. One passenger, Jeremy Glick, told his wife that passengers were talking about trying to stop the hijackers. Later, he told her that the passengers were going to vote on whether or not they should try to break into the cockpit and take control of the plane.

Burnett made one final call to his wife. He told her, “We're going to take back the airplane.” She thought that was a bad idea. She felt they should wait for the authorities to take care of the situation. Burnett said, “We can't wait for the authorities. I don't know what they could do anyway. It's up to us. I think we can do it.”

One passenger had reached an operator for the phone company. He never hung up, and the operator continued listening.

At 9:55 a.m., the operator heard someone say, "Are you guys ready? OK! Let's roll!" Just before 10 a.m., Burnett and other passengers attacked the hijackers. They were flying over rural Pennsylvania. The cockpit recorder caught the sounds of the passengers fighting with the hijackers. The hijackers rocked the plane side to side and up and down to try to stop the passengers. The plane went upside-down. Shortly after 10 a.m., the plane crashed in a field near Shanksville, Pennsylvania. Everyone on board died instantly.

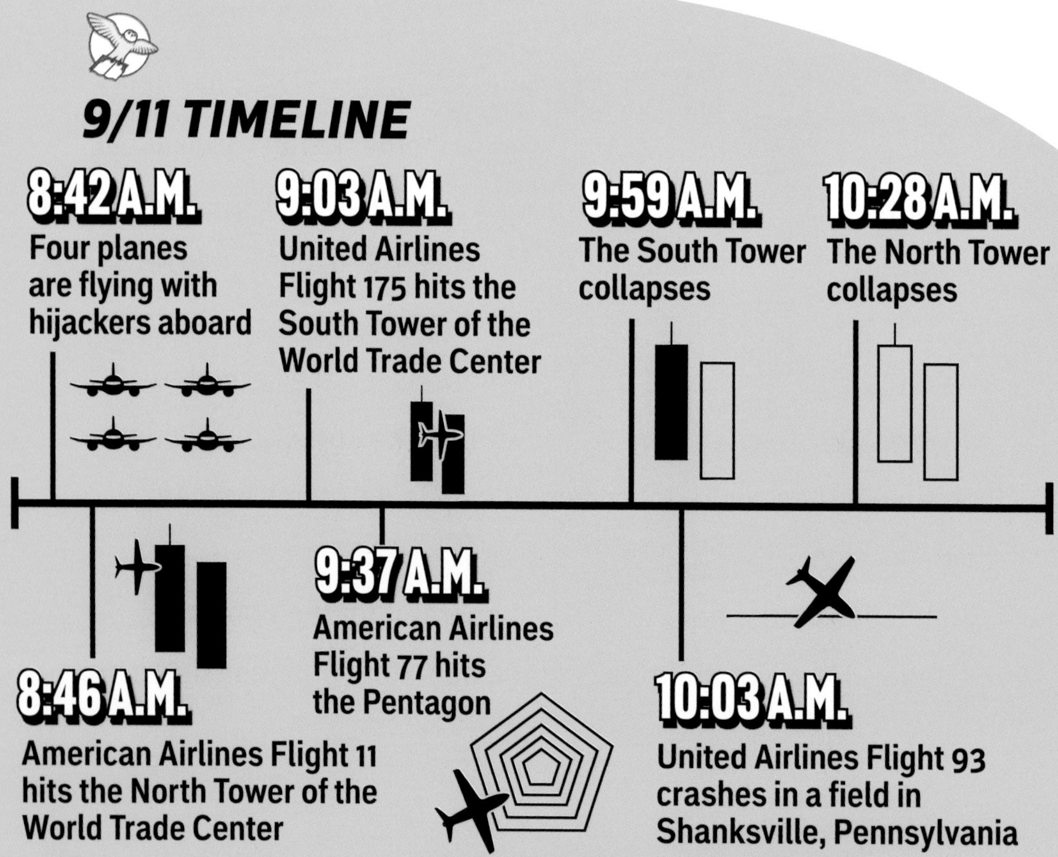

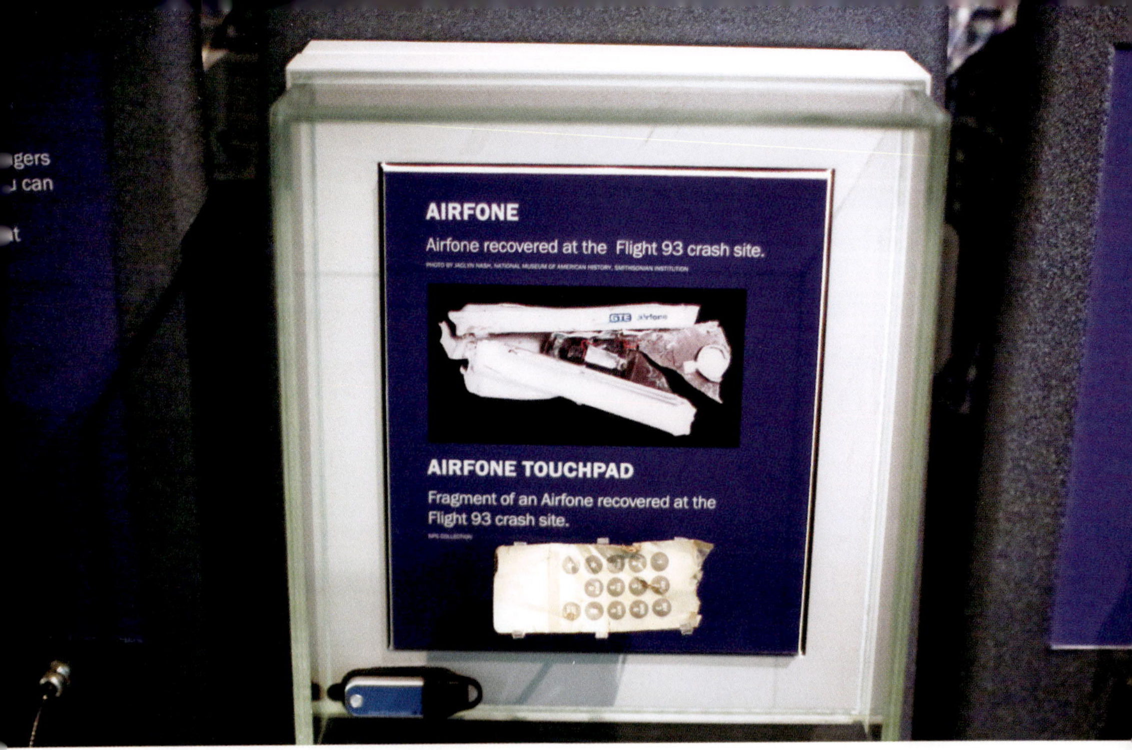

Because Flight 93 did not crash into a building like the other planes did, investigators were able to recover more evidence and wreckage from the plane.

The hijackers were flying toward Washington, DC. The 9/11 Commission later reported that the hijackers would have crashed into either the White House or the US Capitol building, where Congress was in session. Terrorists killed hundreds of people at the Pentagon and World Trade Center. The collapsing buildings killed many more. But in Shanksville, only 40 victims died. That was because Tom Burnett and others worked together to prevent the hijackers from reaching their target. A Federal Bureau of Investigation (FBI) agent later said, "The only victims were them, and they saved countless numbers of lives, destruction, devastation, on a day that already had so many tragedies."

CHAPTER FOUR

MERWYNN PAGDANGANAN

Merwynn Pagdanganan was at work on September 11, 2001. He worked in the Pentagon Clinic. But he was not a medical professional. His job was in information technology (IT). That meant he worked with the computer technology in the clinic.

That morning, as he walked through the Pentagon, he heard that two planes had crashed into the World Trade Center in New York. Half an hour later, he felt something shake the building a little. He was not worried. He knew the Pentagon was being worked on, and he had felt the building shake a little before.

Then, he noticed that the lights in the rooms and hallway were flickering. He realized something was going on that had nothing to do with the construction. He raced back to his office and grabbed an emergency radio. Officials were saying everyone must **evacuate**. Pagdanganan knew it was serious.

The sculptures at the Pentagon Memorial represent the name, age, and location of each victim at the time of the September 11 attacks.

The Pentagon Memorial Chapel was dedicated on the first anniversary of the attacks. It was built where Flight 77 hit the Pentagon.

When he and other employees got outside, there was smoke everywhere. Before, it had been a sunny day with a bright-blue sky. He learned from others that a plane had crashed into the Pentagon.

It was a scary time. No one knew how bad the crash was or whether the building was safe. The building was filling with smoke. Pagdanganan and his coworkers had not been hurt. But they felt wrong leaving others inside. They decided to form teams to go back into the building and help others escape.

US Navy musicians performed at the dedication of the Pentagon Memorial on September 11, 2008.

▲ **The part of the Pentagon damaged in the September 11 attacks was rebuilt.**

Pagdanganan knew the clinic had many patients who would have a hard time leaving on their own. He and another coworker ran into the Pentagon's central courtyard. They set up an area where medical professionals could treat those injured in the crash.

But as they worked to help people either get to medical help or get out of the Pentagon, a voice came over the emergency radio. It said everyone must leave the Pentagon right away. Another plane was coming in their direction. No one knew that Flight 93 would not arrive in Washington, DC, and that there was not more danger to the Pentagon.

"My life changed that day," Pagdanganan said. "I didn't get to talk to my family for almost nine hours. . . . When they finally saw me, they thought they were seeing a ghost." Pagdanganan's family did not want him to return to the Pentagon to work when it reopened. But he felt he had to. One of the biggest things he learned that day was that there are lots of people who are willing to help each other. "We tend to forget what we, as individuals, can do out there if we help each other out," Pagdanganan said. He never forgot that lesson. Ten years after the attacks, he became a volunteer first responder for the county emergency response team. Helping people in emergencies was something he wanted to continue to do.

THINK ABOUT IT

- Many of these citizen heroes had the chance to leave immediately, but they stayed behind or went back to help others. Why do you think that is?
- What are some of the ways you prepare for emergencies in your life? Do you practice fire drills or other safety drills at school? How could your training help you be a citizen hero in a time of need?
- Why do you think the passengers on Flight 93 decided to try to fight the terrorists? Was it the right thing to do? Why or why not?

GLOSSARY

authorities (uh-THOR-ih-tees): The authorities are people who are in charge of a situation, usually a government or the police. Deena Burnett told her husband to let the authorities handle the hijackers.

equities trader (EK-wih-teez TRAY-dur): An equities trader buys and sells stocks on the stock market for a company or its customers. Welles Crowther worked as an equities trader in the World Trade Center.

evacuate (eh-VAK-yoo-ayt): To evacuate a place means to leave it quickly because there may be danger there. The Pentagon employees were ordered to evacuate the building right away.

foxhole (FOX-hole): A foxhole is a small area dug out to protect soldiers from the enemy during a battle. Philip McNair compared escaping the Pentagon on September 11, 2001, to being in a foxhole.

hijacked (HY-jakt): When something has been hijacked, it has been taken over by force. Terrorists hijacked four airplanes on September 11, 2001, to fly them into buildings.

inhalation (in-huh-LAY-shun): Inhalation is material that has been inhaled, or breathed in. Smoke inhalation can be very dangerous for the lungs.

terrorists (TAYR-ur-ists): Terrorists are people who commit violent acts to make people feel fear or terror. The passengers of Flight 93 attacked the terrorists who took over their plane.

volunteer (vah-lunn-TEER): A volunteer is a person who does a job or task without getting paid. Merwynn Pagdanganan became a volunteer first responder ten years after 9/11.

SELECTED BIBLIOGRAPHY

9/11 Memorial Staff. "Remembering the 'Man in the Red Bandana.'" *9/11 Memorial*, n.d., 911memorial.org. Accessed 19 Oct. 2023.

Bustamante, Claudia Sanchez. "'My Life Changed That Day'— DHA Staff Recalls 9/11 at the Pentagon." *Health.mil*, 10 Sept. 2021, health.mil. Accessed 19 Oct. 2023.

"Investigation of United Flight 93." *The FBI*, n.d., fbi.gov. Accessed 19 Oct. 2023.

FIND OUT MORE

BOOKS

Fagan, Honor Crowther. *The Man in the Red Bandanna*. CreateSpace, 2013.

Hamen, Susan E. *Survivors on 9/11*. Parker, CO: The Child's World, 2025.

Platt, Richard. *Stephen Biesty's Incredible Cross Sections of Everything*. New York, NY: DK, 2020.

WEBSITES

Visit our website for links about citizen heroes on 9/11:
childsworld.com/links

Note to Parents, Caregivers, Teachers, and Librarians: We routinely verify our web links to make sure they are safe and active sites. So encourage your readers to check them out!

INDEX